Kids Can Help

KIDS

by Emily Raij

Consultant: Lisa Joyslin, Inclusive Volunteerism Program
Manager, Minnesota Association for Volunteer Administration,
St. Paul, Minnesota

CAPSTONE PRESS
a capstone imprint

Capstone Captivate is published by Capstone Press, an imprint of Capstone.
1710 Roe Crest Drive
North Mankato, Minnesota 56003
www.capstonepub.com

Library of Congress Cataloging-in-Publication Data is available on the Library of Congress website.
ISBN 978-1-4966-8377-9 (library binding)
ISBN 978-1-4966-8783-8 (paperback)
ISBN 978-1-4966-8428-8 (ebook pdf)

Summary: Make the world a better place for kids! This book is full of ideas and projects readers can put into action to help with racial justice and human rights.

Image Credits
Alamy: MITO images GmbH, 12; AP Photo: The Messenger-Inquirer/Alan Warren, 22; iStockphoto: FatCamera, 6, 27, fstop123, 5, 9, kali9, 16, 26, lisegagne, 13, SDI Productions, 28, 29, Steex, 14; Pixabay: DavidZydd (stripe background), 1 and throughout; Shutterstock: Alex_Traksel, 25, Christopher Penler, 24, ESB Professional, 21, iyd39, 23 (top), Jamie Lamor Thompson, 15, Krolja (hand), 8 (bottom), 23 (bottom), michaeljung, 20, Monkey Business Images, cover, 8 (top), Rawpixel, back cover, 18, Roberto Galan, 19, Vince360, 11, wavebreakmedia, 17

Editorial Credits
Editor: Erika L. Shores; Designers: Sara Radka and Elyse White; Media Researcher: Svetlana Zhurkin; Production Specialist: Tori Abraham

All internet sites appearing in back matter were available and accurate when this book was sent to press.

Words in **bold** are in the glossary.

Printed in the United States of America.
PA117

TABLE OF CONTENTS

Caring for Each Other 4

What Can I Do? 8

Service Projects 12

What If I Want to Do More? 24

Rights for Everyone 26

Other Ways to Get Involved 28

Glossary 30

Read More 31

Internet Sites 31

Index 32

Caring for Each Other

Take a look around your school. Think about your neighbors. Is everyone the same? Were you all born in the same city or even country? The answer to both questions is probably no. People come from different places. They speak different languages. They have different **ethnicities**. They believe different things. They have different types of families. They have different abilities, or things they can do. But all people have the same human rights. These are the rights all people deserve. Food, shelter, and safety are all human rights.

Human rights need to be respected everywhere. This includes at work, at school, and in the community. Laws should also respect and protect people's human rights. That means everyone is treated fairly. Kids have human rights too. And kids can stand up for each other.

» Classmates can be different in many ways, but everyone has the same rights.

» If someone has been treated unkindly, you
can find ways to show that person you care.

Everyone has the same human rights. But not everyone is treated the same all the time. Sometimes people are treated differently because of where they were born. Other times people are treated differently because of what they look like or what they believe. That is not right. You can speak up if you see someone being treated unfairly or unkindly. You may see an **unjust** law or school rule that isn't fair to some people. You can say something.

Getting involved shows you care about other people. You can help make sure people's rights are respected. But you don't have to solve the whole problem to be a hero. You can help in small ways too. You can use your abilities to help find answers and work with others.

What Can I Do?

Think about ways you like to help. You can use what you like doing to help other kids. You might find that your gift for writing comes in handy for some projects. If you're a good artist, that skill can be useful too.

» A charity might have volunteers who serve food to people in need.

HELPING FACT
More than 62 million people volunteer in the United States each year.

» Volunteers can gather donations to give to people who need food.

Sometimes people need help meeting their needs. **Charities** are groups that take care of immediate needs, such as having food and a safe place to live. These groups may collect money to help people. You can help a charity raise money. Or you can **volunteer** directly with the people who need help. That might mean giving them things they need to be fed and to be safe.

Sometimes there are bigger reasons why people's needs aren't being met. Maybe there are unfair laws and **policies**. These may leave out certain people. They may cause people to be treated unfairly. Some policies keep people from getting **access** to the same things as others. That could include schools or jobs. Other policies may punish one group of people more than another.

Human rights **activists** try to change laws and policies that are unfair or hurt people. Activists want to make the world safe and fair for all. You can be one too. Make your community a place where everyone is treated fairly. Work with others to make your school a safe, welcoming place.

» Activists walk down a street holding signs. They want to bring attention to an unfair policy.

Service Projects

MAKE YOUR SCHOOL WELCOMING TO ALL

New students can always use a friend. Create a new student welcome bag for your class. It can include a book with photos and names of all the students in your class. This gives new students an easy way to learn names and friendly faces. You can also put in photos of everyday school activities, such as lunch, recess, and library time.

» The first few days at a new school can be scary.

» Taking time to help a new student is a good way
to make your school a caring place.

Include some information you think the new
student would need to get to know your school or
town. Look for books or magazines about your city, a
list of fun things to do, and a calendar of events such
as town festivals or plays. Make a list of places such as
the library and parks that a new student would want
to know about. Did your teacher tell you about the
new student? If so, find some books from your school
library that may interest him or her.

MAKING YOUR SCHOOL LIBRARY WELCOMING TO ALL

Kids should be able to see themselves in the books they read. Do the people in the books in your school library and classroom look like all the students at your school? If not, talk to your teacher and school librarian to see what books might be missing.

» You can ask your librarian to read books about all kinds of people from all kinds of places.

Marley's Mission

Marley Dias was 11 years old when she decided she was tired of reading about mostly white boys and dogs in books at her school. She wanted to see books with black girls like her as the main characters. Marley set a goal of collecting 1,000 books with black girls as the main characters. She found many more and created the #1,000BlackGirlBooks campaign. Marley even wrote a book for other kids working for change.

Ask These Questions When Choosing Books:

- Do the books have characters from different ethnicities, places, genders, and other groups?

- Are they written and illustrated by **diverse** authors and illustrators?

- Do the books share stories written by many different kinds of people, including people who have had the experiences they write about?

- Do the books show everyday people, not just famous people?

- Do the books show people who are rarely talked about or "invisible" in books? These are people who live in rural areas, service workers, people with disabilities, families with two dads or two moms, families with single moms or dads, and homeless families.

» Making immigrant students feel welcome helps them get
used to their new life.

Some new students come from far away. **Immigrants**
are people who have moved from one country to another.
Many people leave countries where they have few rights.
They do not have access to good schools or jobs. They may
worry about their safety. Many immigrants come to the
United States seeking a better life for their families.

You can make immigrant students and their families feel welcome. Create posters and signs to hang around school that welcome new students in their own languages. Write welcoming messages that show you're glad they're here. A parent or teacher can help you put together lists of people new families can ask for help, such as counselors and **translators**. A map of the school and lists of school events and other ways for families to get involved are also useful.

Is Your Classroom Welcoming?

- Are there labels on furniture and common items in the room in both English and languages of the new students?

- Are there dictionaries in both English and other languages?

- Does the classroom setup allow everyone, including students who use a wheelchair, to move around easily and sit together?

- Are new students paired with buddies?

Part of respecting people's rights is showing you appreciate where they come from. Celebrate diversity at your school! Work with teachers to hold an **international** festival at school. It will celebrate the many backgrounds of students. Groups of students can share traditions and serve food from their home countries. They can talk about the countries their families are from. Students can also choose countries they want to learn more about.

» You can work with your class and teacher to plan a festival to celebrate different traditions.

» Students at a festival might wear special clothing from the countries their families came from.

There are many things to keep in mind when planning a big event like this. Decide where and when the festival should be. Ask parents and teachers to help set up and clean up. Think about special equipment needed, such as microphones and speakers. You can also make posters to spread the word.

SPREAD KINDNESS

Everyone should feel safe at school. Start a kindness club to show that kindness is important at your school. Talk to teachers or counselors who can help lead the meetings. One club activity can be making kindness posters to hang around the school. Messages can include "Choose kindness" and "All are welcome here."

Set up meetings to talk about other ways to be kind. Think about how to make everyone feel included and prevent bullying. Consider putting an idea box in a common area at school. Students and teachers can give ideas. They can also write notes about times they spotted kids being kind at school. These notes can be read during morning announcements each week.

» You can start a group at school to make
posters reminding each other to be kind.

Finding Out About Autism

Children who have physical and developmental
disabilities should feel welcome at school. Daniel
Stefanski was 14 when he wrote a book called *How
to Talk to an Autistic Kid*. Daniel has **autism**. He
wanted to help kids without autism get to know kids
like him. In the book, he explains some behaviors
children with autism might show, such as repeating
themselves or not making eye contact.

Have you ever seen a student sitting alone at lunch or recess? You can help make sure no one feels lonely at school. That's what first grader Christian Bucks wanted to do at his school in Pennsylvania. He saw a picture of a Buddy Bench at a school in Germany. A Buddy Bench is a place any student can sit when feeling lonely. Christian asked his principal if his school could get a Buddy Bench. The principal thought it was a great idea.

» A classmate who needs a friend during recess might sit on a Buddy Bench.

HELPING FACT

Some schools even collect bottle caps that can be recycled to make the benches. It takes 400 pounds (181 kilograms) of bottle caps to make one bench.

Buddy Benches are usually put on playgrounds. When other students see someone sitting on the bench, they can go over and talk or play. The bench can also be used to show teachers a student is being bullied. Ask your teacher or school principal what you can do to get a Buddy Bench at your school.

What If I Want to Do More?

Laws and policies are not always fair. But they can be changed. Activists work to change these unjust practices. They want to solve the cause of a problem. A human rights activist might **protest** a policy that is unfair to a group of people. These groups may be immigrants, people of color, or people with disabilities.

» Activists hold signs that tell other people they care about immigrants and their rights.

» Writing letters to leaders can let them
know you care about human rights.

You do not have to be loud to make your voice heard.
Call or write to lawmakers to discuss practices that go
against people's human rights. Suggest changes or new
policies to protect immigrants, people with disabilities,
and other groups that need support. Send a letter to the
editor of your local newspaper. Post on social media
with a parent's OK. Pass out information at town events.
Activists make other people aware of a problem. They
help others take action. Activism can change people's
lives in your town and all over the world.

Rights for Everyone

Human rights are everyone's rights. And making sure all people are treated fairly and with respect can be everyone's fight. We can ask for better policies and make real changes. Whether you want to welcome new students at school or welcome new immigrants to the country, there is a project for you. Find one that makes good use of your time and talent. Work for what you care about. Think about what you like to do. You can help on your own or with a group. No act of help is too small when it comes to being kind and including others.

» You show you care when you treat everyone with kindness.

» Classmates can work together to make their
school a place where everyone is welcome.

Other Ways to Get Involved

» Volunteer to pack food or serve a meal at a food pantry or homeless shelter in your town.

» Work with a group to hold a school supply drive for kids whose families may have a hard time paying for these items.

» Set up an Appreciation Station in the school lunchroom. Have students write notes to teachers, custodians, the principal, the school nurse, and other staff thanking them for all they do for you. Pass the notes out each week.

» Start a "Caught You Being Kind" program for students. If you see a student helping someone else or simply showing extra kindness, write the student's name and act of kindness on a note. Notes can be given to the principal to read out loud to the entire school.

» Invite a new student to play at recess, sit with you at lunch, or come to your house for dinner.

» Put together a welcome basket for a new neighbor. Include a nice note, menus from local restaurants, and a treat.

» Start a diverse books club with other students. Your school librarian can help put together a list of books to read. Then students can create written or video book reviews to share. Written reviews can be put into a book kept in the school library. Video reviews can be shown on the school news or website.

Glossary

access (AK-sess)—to make use of something

activist (AC-tiv-ist)—a person who works for social or political change

autism (AW-tiss-uhm)—a condition that causes people to have trouble communicating and forming relationships with others

charity (CHAYR-uh-tee)—a group that raises money or collects goods to help those in need

diverse (dye-VURSS)—varied or assorted; when a group of people are diverse, they may be different ethnicities, have different abilities, or have different talents or skills

ethnicity (eth-NI-suh-tee)—a group of people who share the same language, traditions, and culture

immigrant (IM-uh-gruhnt)—a person who leaves one country and settles in another

international (in-tur-NASH-uh-nuhl)—including more than one nation; between or among the nations of the world

policy (POL-uh-see)—a general plan that people use to help them make decisions or take action

protest (pro-TEST)—to speak out about something strongly and publicly

translator (TRANZ-lay-tuhr)—a person who changes words from one language to another

unjust (un-JUHST)—not fair

volunteer (vol-uhn-TIHR)—to offer to do something without pay

Read More

Dias, Marley. *Marley Dias Gets It Done: And So Can You!* New York: Scholastic Press, 2018.

Ganeri, Anita. *Racism.* North Mankato, MN: Picture Window Books, 2020.

Hudson, Wade and Cheryl Willis Hudson. *We Rise, We Resist, We Raise Our Voices.* New York: Crown Books for Young Readers, 2018.

Internet Sites

Meet Young Immigrants
teacher.scholastic.com/activities/immigration/young_immigrants/

Random Acts of Kindness
randomactsofkindness.org/kindness-ideas

Index

abilities, 4, 7

activists, 10, 24, 25

activities, 12

autism, 21

books, 13, 14, 15

Bucks, Christian, 22

Buddy Benches, 22, 23

bullying, 20, 23

charities, 9

Dias, Marley, 15

disabilities, 15, 17, 21, 24, 25

diverse books, 14, 15, 29

diverse books clubs, 29

diversity, 14, 15, 18

ethnicities, 4, 15

human rights, 4, 7, 10, 16, 25, 26

immigrants, 16, 17, 24, 26

international festivals, 18, 19

kindness clubs, 20, 28

languages, 4, 17

lawmakers, 25

laws, 4, 7, 10, 24

letter writing, 25

new students, 12, 13, 16, 17, 26, 29

policies, 10, 24, 25, 26

projects, 8, 26

protests, 24

rules, 7

schools, 16, 18, 20, 21, 22, 23, 26

school supply drives, 28

Stefanski, Daniel, 21

volunteering, 9, 28